GREAT ENTREPRENEURS
IN U.S. HISTORY

John Pierpont Morgan

and the Banking Industry

David Machajewski

PowerKids
press.

New York

Published in 2017 by The Rosen Publishing Group, Inc.
29 East 21st Street, New York, NY 10010

First Edition

Editor: Sarah Machajewski
Book Design: Mickey Harmon

Photo Credits: Cover, pp. 1–4, 6–10, 12, 14–24, 26–32 (series design) Melodist/Shutterstock.com; cover (J. P. Morgan) Museum of the City of New York/Contributor/Archive Photos/Getty Images; pp. 5, 23 Hulton Archive/Stringer/Hulton Archive/Getty Images; p. 7 Universal History Archive/Universal Images Group/Getty Images; p. 8 https://commons.wikimedia.org/wiki/File:Junius_Spencer_Morgan.png; p. 9 https://commons.wikimedia.org/wiki/File:English_High_School_-_403002054_-_City_of_Boston_Archives.jpg; p. 11 https://en.wikipedia.org/wiki/J._P._Morgan#/media/File:JP_Morgan.jpg; pp. 13, 15, 16 Image courtesy of the Library of Congress; p. 17 https://en.wikipedia.org/wiki/J._P._Morgan#/media/File:JPMorganLibrary.jpg; p. 19 New York Daily News/Contributor/New York Daily News/Getty Images; p. 21 William England/London Stereoscopic Company/Getty Images; p. 25 Jeffrey Zeldman/Flickr.com; p 27 Everett Historical/Shutterstock.com; p. 29 https://commons.wikimedia.org/wiki/File:J.P._Morgan,_Mausoleum,_Hartford,_Connecticut,_1913,_Agence_Rol,_BNF_Gallica.jpg.

Cataloging-in-Publication Data

Names: Machajewski, David.
Title: John Pierpont Morgan and the banking industry / David Machajewski.
Description: New York : PowerKids Press, 2017. | Series: Great entrepreneurs in U.S. history | Includes index.
Identifiers: ISBN 9781499421279 (pbk.) | ISBN 9781499421293 (library bound) | ISBN 9781499421286 (6 pack)
Subjects: LCSH: Morgan, J. Pierpont (John Pierpont), 1837-1913–Juvenile literature.) | Bankers–United States–Biography–Juvenile literature.) | Capitalists and financiers–United States–Biography–Juvenile literature.
Classification: LCC HG2463.M6 M23 2017 | DDC 332.1'092–d23

Manufactured in the United States of America

CPSIA Compliance Information: Batch #BS16PK: For Further Information contact Rosen Publishing, New York, New York at 1-800-237-9932

Contents

A Captain of Industry

All modern **technology**—from the light bulb to computers—began as great ideas dreamed up by inventors and engineers. However, you need more than just a person to bring a great idea to life. You also need money!

Behind every great invention is a person who knows how to turn it into a business. Owners of new businesses often borrow money from banks and **investors** to get started before they can make money on their own.

John Pierpont Morgan, or J. P. Morgan, was one of the most famous bankers and investors in history. He was a powerful man who controlled a lot of **capital**, and he started a private bank that helped develop many new technologies. Whether the technology focused on motors, lamps, steel, or railroads, Morgan's wealth helped many businesses that drove America into the future.

J. P. Morgan was one of the most powerful men of his day. Considered a master of finance, he remains one of the most famous bankers and businessmen in history.

5

Early Life

John Pierpont Morgan was born April 17, 1837, in Hartford, Connecticut. The Morgans were a **prominent** New England family. His father, Junius Spencer Morgan, was a banker, and he came from a long line of successful businessmen. His mother was the daughter of the Reverend John Pierpont, a minister, activist, and poet. Morgan, who went by the name Pierpont, was the oldest child in his family. He had three sisters and a brother who passed away at age 11.

Morgan learned a lot from both his grandfathers. He attended church every Sunday with his grandfather Joseph Morgan, and he loved to sing hymns. At school, he stood out as a natural leader among his classmates. His father realized that Morgan had great **potential** to follow in his footsteps as a successful businessman, and he raised him with discipline.

Morgan's Childhood

While he was a happy and outgoing child, Morgan was also sickly and often had to miss school. He spent a lot of time alone, and he enjoyed playing the card game solitaire to relax. As a young boy, Morgan visited many art galleries and attended concerts with his family. This was the beginning of a lifelong passion for the arts. Later in life, he was known for having a large and impressive art collection, which he first began assembling as a child.

This building is the Connecticut State Capitol as it appeared in the 1800s.

In His Father's Footsteps

When Morgan was about 14, he entered English High School in Boston, Massachusetts. Shortly after his graduation, Junius Morgan accepted a job at the bank George Peabody and Company in London. In 1854, the Morgan family moved to England. J. P. Morgan attended schools in Switzerland and Germany, where he learned French and German and showed a talent for mathematics.

Junius Spencer Morgan was an important businessman in his own right, and his partnership with his son was key to J. P. Morgan's success.

English High School in Boston

In 1857, when Morgan was 20 years old, he left Europe to begin his career in banking. His father had arranged a job for him in New York City as an accountant with Duncan, Sherman and Company, which was the American representative of his father's company. This business connection between Morgan and his father from the United States to England would prove to be very important for America's future.

Climbing the Banking Ladder

In his first job, Morgan was organized and detail-oriented. He was able to do math quickly, he spent long hours at the bank, and he was very committed to his work. He soon gained a strong reputation in the banking world. The **partners** of his firm recognized his great potential, and it was clear to them that Morgan had excellent business instincts.

In the early years of his career, Morgan had big ideas about new business opportunities. He often wrote letters to his father about business and life in New York City. At this time, he made many important friends. He was often a guest in the homes of powerful New York families, and these high society connections helped him advance his banking career.

J. P. Morgan made a strong impression on most people he met. He was driven to achieve greatness from an early age, and he was determined to make his mark on the world.

A Striking Appearance

J. P. Morgan had a medical condition called rosacea, which caused his skin to be discolored. He also had a condition that caused his nose to swell. Morgan hated being photographed, and he sometimes demanded that pictures of himself be altered, or changed, to downplay the look of his nose. He was known for having a strong, powerful presence in person. A bishop who once met Morgan stated that his visit made him feel "as if a [very strong wind] had blown through the house."

From Old World to New World

Between 1861 and 1871, J. P. Morgan worked for his father's banking company in New York and for the Dabney, Morgan and Company firm. In 1871, Junius Morgan crafted a deal in which his banking company took ownership of another. J. P. Morgan then became a partner in the new firm, Drexel, Morgan and Company. This company, which later became J. P. Morgan and Company, soon became one of the most powerful banks in the world.

Morgan's father's job gave him access to very rich European bankers and investors in London. The two men worked together to bring capital overseas to support American industry. In the 1800s, the United States was a young but fast-growing country. As new technology began to develop, foreign money supported the building of many new and important businesses.

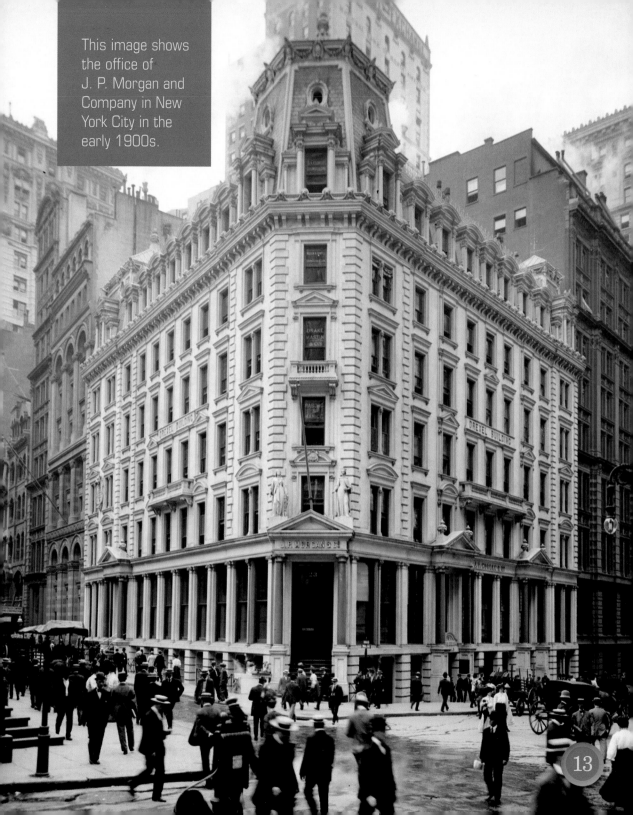

This image shows the office of J. P. Morgan and Company in New York City in the early 1900s.

13

A Man of Many Industries

J. P. Morgan's rise as a banker happened at the same time the American economy began to grow. As Morgan brought capital from Europe to the United States, he would travel to London every year to work with his partners there. All the while, Morgan's many financial **ventures** earned him a great amount of wealth.

As an investment banker, Morgan put his wealth into stocks, which means that he paid to own parts of companies. With his money in several different types of businesses, he helped fund the Edison Electric Company and bought many railroads, eventually becoming one of the most powerful railroad owners in the world. He also bought many steel companies, which he turned into the biggest steel producer in the United States.

Electricity, Steel, and More

J. P. Morgan is remembered for consolidating businesses. This means he bought many smaller businesses and turned them into one giant business. He joined the Edison General Electric and Thomson-Houston Electric Company to form General Electric, a company that is still one of the world's biggest electrical equipment manufacturers. He also merged his own Federal Steel Company with the Carnegie Steel Company and others to form United States Steel Corporation, the world's first billion-dollar corporation. Morgan did the same with farm equipment companies and shipping companies.

Andrew Carnegie, another great entrepreneur, founded the Carnegie Steel Company, shown here. Morgan bought Carnegie's company in 1901 for $480 million. When the deal was done, Morgan reportedly said, "Congratulations, Mr. Carnegie, you are now the richest man in the world."

Iron Horses

J. P. Morgan first began working with the railroad industry in 1885 when he struck a deal between the New York Central Railroad and the Pennsylvania Railroad, two of the biggest railroads in the United States. He formed a partnership that eliminated competition between them because the competition

As one of the world's most powerful railroad businessmen, J. P. Morgan controlled about 5,000 miles (8,047 km) of American railroads by 1902.

An Impressive Art Collection

J. P. Morgan was interested in more than just business, and he is remembered as one of the greatest art collectors of his time. He was determined to have the world's greatest art collection and owned pieces from ancient Greece, Egypt, and more. By 1902, he had collected so many pieces of art that they no longer fit in his home! He built a private library to house them, and he donated many items to the Metropolitan Museum of Art in New York City.

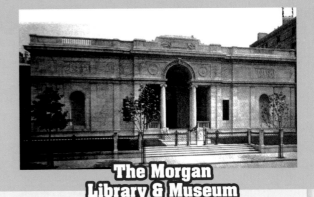
The Morgan Library & Museum

could have hurt American shipping and travel. Morgan did similar work in 1886 with two other big railroads.

Morgan's influence and experience in the railroad industry was so strong that he was asked to fix many of the biggest railroads in the country in 1893, when there was a financial panic in America. The businesses behind these railroads, which included the Northern Pacific, the Erie Railroad, and the Southern Railroad, had become unstable due to problems with the American economy. Morgan's work helped make them stable again.

J. P. Morgan at Home

J. P. Morgan met his first wife, Amelia Sturges, in 1858 while he was still a young banker. Known to Morgan by her nickname "Mimi," Sturges was the daughter of a wealthy New York family. The couple married in 1861, but Sturges died of a sickness called tuberculosis just four months after their wedding. Losing Mimi was very difficult for Morgan. He hired the best doctors and did everything in his power to save her life, but he couldn't.

Throughout his life, Morgan remained very involved in his church. It was at church that he met his second wife, Frances Louisa Tracy, the daughter of a New York lawyer, in 1865. Together, they had three daughters and a son, Jack, who was **groomed** to follow in Morgan's footsteps in the same way Morgan had followed his father.

A Banker at Sea

In his adult life, J. P. Morgan developed an interest in sailing, and it became one of his favorite hobbies. He had a 165-foot (50 m) yacht, or large boat, named the *Corsair*, where he often held private business meetings. Around the time his father passed away, Morgan bought one of the largest luxury boats of the time. In 1912, Morgan had purchased a ticket for the *Titanic's* first voyage, but he was unable to attend because of an illness.

J. P. Morgan reads to his children.

Wall Street and the White House

By the time J. P. Morgan helped stabilize the railroad industry in 1893, his wealth, influence, and reputation for handling brilliant business deals had grown to huge proportions. He was one of the most powerful men in America.

By 1895, a **depression** hit the American economy. It **depleted** the U.S. government's gold reserve. Morgan thought of a plan to help the government, but it was also an opportunity to make a profit. Morgan worked with President Grover Cleveland and led a deal with foreign investors to resupply the United States' gold reserve.

Morgan's actions saved the U.S. government and prevented the U.S. dollar from collapsing. Many people saw him as a hero. However, his ability to bail out the government shocked many. Some criticized his power.

J. P. Morgan led a group that helped the U.S. Treasury (pictured here in 1859) by supplying $62 million in gold to back the country's currency. Morgan said it was his proudest accomplishment.

Protecting the Little Guy

By the early 1900s, J. P. Morgan was at the peak of his power. While he did many good things for the economy with his money, many Americans were concerned with his **monopolies** and unchecked control over many industries. Morgan's influence even helped William McKinley, who was friendly to big business, become president in 1897. But after President McKinley was shot and killed in 1901, and with the American public growing more suspicious of businessmen like Morgan, things started to change.

Theodore Roosevelt, who became president in 1901, set out to control the unchecked power of big business in order to protect the American public. Roosevelt was able to successfully break up J. P. Morgan's railroad monopoly. This setback angered Morgan, but he was still determined to grow his businesses.

Andrew Carnegie.
Steel King.

Pierpont Morgan.
Trust King.

William Rockefeller.
Oil King.

This is a political cartoon showing three "kings" of industry in J. P. Morgan's day. As this cartoon shows, Morgan's critics thought he had too much power.

The Morgan Library

Later in life, J. P. Morgan had more time to explore his interests in traveling and collecting art and books. He had collected so many treasures from around the world that he decided to build a private library in New York City to display them. The library, which is now called the Morgan Library & Museum, was built between 1902 and 1906. During this time, Morgan also made many large donations and built monuments in places such Harvard University and his hometown of Hartford, Connecticut.

Morgan had always wished for the library to be available for people to use. In 1924, Morgan's son made one of the largest cultural donations in U.S. history when he made the library open to the public. The Morgan Library & Museum remains an active and important historical museum to this day.

The Morgan Library & Museum was built next to Morgan's private home in Manhattan.

Morgan's Grand Finale

In 1907, another financial panic hit the American economy. For the second time, the U.S. government called upon Morgan to save it from financial collapse. Morgan's former enemy Theodore Roosevelt wanted him to use the government's money to stabilize the economy. Morgan then called a meeting of the leaders of the most powerful businesses in the country. During this meeting, Morgan locked the leaders in a room overnight and played solitaire while they talked about the plan he had developed.

Eventually, Morgan convinced the bankers and financial leaders to invest their resources to stabilize the economy, improve public **confidence**, and bail out the government to prevent a financial collapse. This event was very important, and many people celebrated J. P. Morgan as a hero for stopping a major economic disaster—again.

Theodore Roosevelt

With a financial crisis close at hand, President Roosevelt turned to J. P. Morgan to help fix the American economy. Roosevelt is pictured here with his cabinet.

J. P. Morgan's Legacy

After rescuing the American economy for a second and final time, J. P. Morgan half retired and focused more on his travels and his art collection. He died on March 31, 1913, at the age of 75. On the day of his funeral in April 1913, the New York Stock Exchange closed in his honor for a half day—a very rare occasion.

J. P. Morgan was a great entrepreneur, and his **legacy** is important. Today, his banking company still exists as JPMorgan Chase & Co., and it's the largest bank in the United States. As one of the greatest art collectors of his day, he donated many important works of art to public museums. Without J. P. Morgan, life, finance, and government in the United States might have been very different.

J. P. Morgan was buried in his hometown of Hartford, Connecticut.

A Timeline of J. P. Morgan's Life

1837 — John Pierpont Morgan is born in Hartford, Connecticut.

1857 — After completing his studies in Europe, Morgan begins his career as an accountant in New York City.

1861 — Morgan becomes the agent for his father's London banking company in New York City.

1871 — Morgan becomes a partner in the New York City banking firm Drexel, Morgan and Company.

1885 — Morgan begins organizing railroads.

1891 — Morgan organizes the merger of Edison General Electric and Thomson-Houston Electric Company to create General Electric.

1893 — A financial panic disrupts the railroad industry. Morgan is asked to help fix the problem.

1895 — Morgan becomes senior partner of Drexel, Morgan and Company. The firm is renamed J. P. Morgan and Company.

1901 — Morgan purchases the Carnegie Steel Company and merges it with the Federal Steel Company and others to create the world's first billion-dollar corporation.

1907 — Morgan leads the effort to solve the financial crisis of 1907.

1913 — Morgan dies at the age of 75 in Rome, Italy.

Glossary

capital: Financial resources used to generate wealth.

confidence: The state of feeling certain about something.

deplete: To use up the supply of something.

depression: A period when a country's economy is slow, business is going poorly, and many people are out of work

groomed: Prepared or trained.

investor: A person who gives money to a business in order to make more money later.

legacy: Something that comes from someone in the past.

monopoly: Complete control by a person or organization over all of the businesses in a certain industry.

partner: A person who takes part in a business with other people.

prominent: Important or famous.

potential: Qualities that may be developed and lead to success in the future.

technology: The use of science to solve problems and the tools used to solve those problems.

venture: A business opportunity that involves risk.

Index

Websites

Due to the changing nature of Internet links, PowerKids Press has developed an online list of websites related to the subject of this book. This site is updated regularly. Please use this link to access the list: www.powerkidslinks.com/entre/morg